Elephants
and other
amazing animals

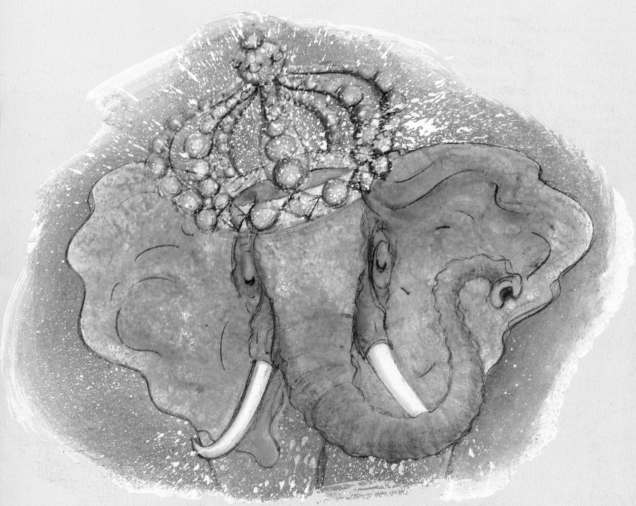

Compiled by Wendy Body and Pat Edwards

Acknowledgements

Macdonald & Co. (Publishers) Ltd for the short stories 'The Cock and the Dragon' and 'The First Story of Anansi the Spider' from pp.14-15, 56-57 *Fabulous Beasts* by Richard Blythe (1977); the author's representatives for the poem 'My little pet spider' by John Kirkby from *New Essex Poets Present 'The Rainbow Said That He Wouldn't Get Up' and Other Poems* by Harlow Young Poets; Faber and Faber Ltd for the story 'How The Elephant Became' from *How The Whale Became* by Ted Hughes; New Zealand Department of Education for the story 'The Taniwha' by Cathie Penetito, first published as 'Te Taniwah o Whangaparaoa' by New Zealand Department of Education, Copyright 1974 Cathie Penetito. Pages 12-13 and 52-53 were written by David Jamieson; pages 18-25 and 62 were written by Bill Boyle.

We are grateful to the following for permission to reproduce photographs: J. Allen Cash, pp.10-11(3); Geri Kuster, pp.52-53(5); Martina Selway, pp.12.

Illustrators, other than those acknowledged with each story, include: Maggi Baker p.9; Antonia Enthoven pp.22-25; Charles Front pp.62-64; Joanna Graham pp.4-8; Robert Jahnke pp.54-61; Alan Jane pp.48-49; Judy Leech pp.26-46; Robert Mancini p.47; Ian Penney pp.14-17; Bryna Waldman pp.18-21; David Woodward pp.50-51.

Contents

Anansi and Snake

The First Story of Anansi the Spider

Anansi the Spider is famous among children in Africa. There are many funny stories about him, because he is such a clever spider, and full of tricks. The stories are called Anansi Stories, but it was not always so. This is how they got their name.

"Anansi is grumbling again," said Dog. "He says all the animals have things named after them, but nothing is named after him."

"Anansi is so weak and silly," said Tiger. "Why should anything be named after him? Fancy Tiger Lilies being named after *him*."

"Or Tiger Stories," said Dog.

"Ah, a lot of things are named after me," said Tiger. "I am the strongest animal, that is why."

"Tiger Stories are *famous*!" cried Dog.

"Quite right," said Tiger.

Anansi the Spider crept up to them. "Oh, please, Tiger," he said, in his silkiest voice. "Just because I am weak you all laugh at me. Please let the stories be named after me."

"Snakes alive!" exclaimed Dog, quite shocked.

Tiger pricked up his ears. "All right, Anansi," he jeered, "you *shall* have my stories named after you. But only if you bring me Snake. Bring me Snake – alive!"

5

"Oh dear!" said Anansi. "He bites! But all right, I will try." And all the other animals laughed and laughed as Anansi plodded off.

He went to Snake's hole and right in front of it he dug a pit.

"I know you are trying to catch me," said Snake, wrapping his tail round a tree so that he would not fall in. "But I am not silly." And he came out of his hole, slid round the pit and went for a walk.

6

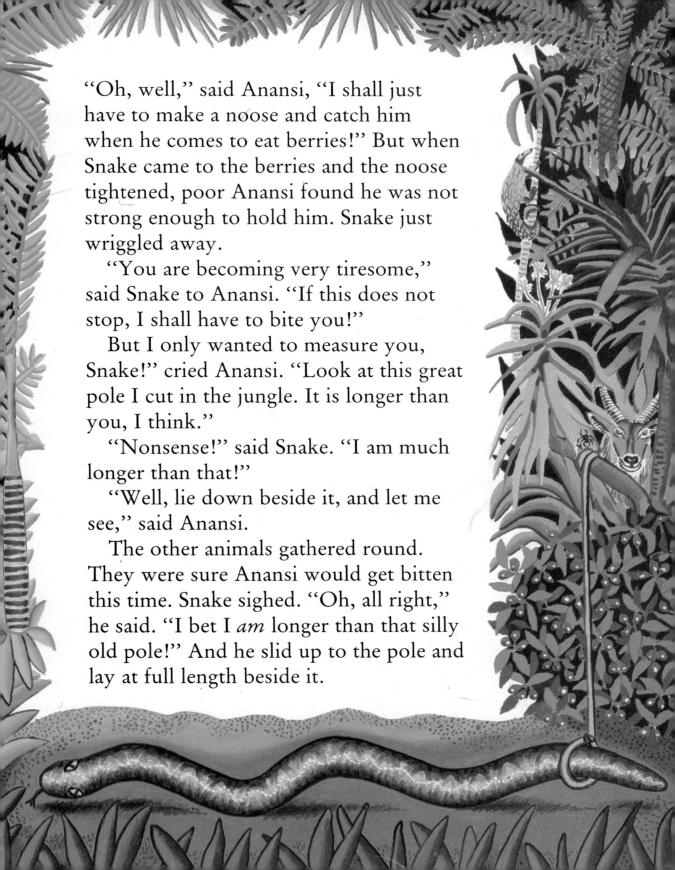

"Oh, well," said Anansi, "I shall just have to make a noose and catch him when he comes to eat berries!" But when Snake came to the berries and the noose tightened, poor Anansi found he was not strong enough to hold him. Snake just wriggled away.

"You are becoming very tiresome," said Snake to Anansi. "If this does not stop, I shall have to bite you!"

But I only wanted to measure you, Snake!" cried Anansi. "Look at this great pole I cut in the jungle. It is longer than you, I think."

"Nonsense!" said Snake. "I am much longer than that!"

"Well, lie down beside it, and let me see," said Anansi.

The other animals gathered round. They were sure Anansi would get bitten this time. Snake sighed. "Oh, all right," he said. "I bet I *am* longer than that silly old pole!" And he slid up to the pole and lay at full length beside it.

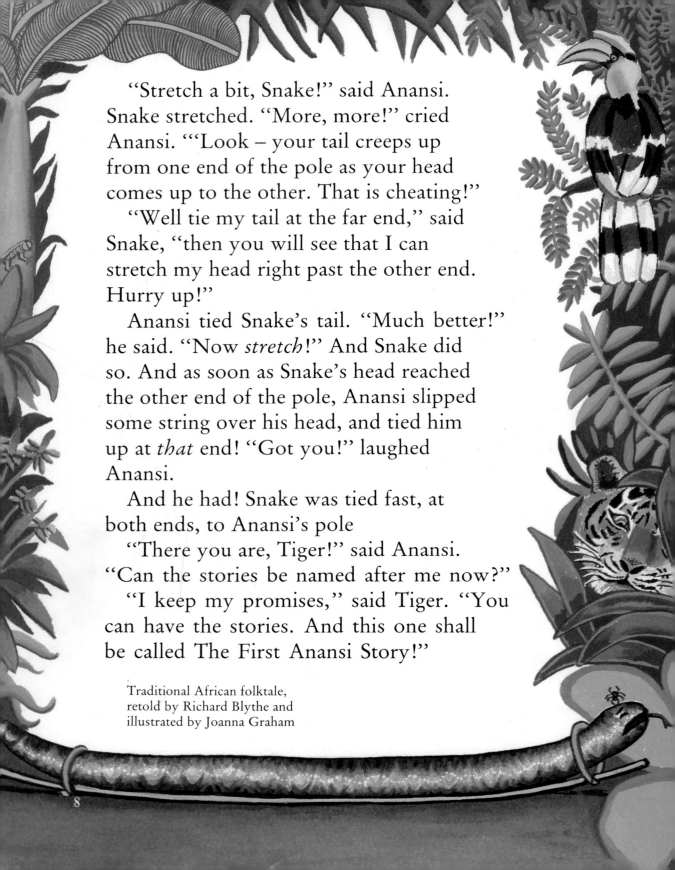

"Stretch a bit, Snake!" said Anansi. Snake stretched. "More, more!" cried Anansi. "'Look – your tail creeps up from one end of the pole as your head comes up to the other. That is cheating!"

"Well tie my tail at the far end," said Snake, "then you will see that I can stretch my head right past the other end. Hurry up!"

Anansi tied Snake's tail. "Much better!" he said. "Now *stretch*!" And Snake did so. And as soon as Snake's head reached the other end of the pole, Anansi slipped some string over his head, and tied him up at *that* end! "Got you!" laughed Anansi.

And he had! Snake was tied fast, at both ends, to Anansi's pole

"There you are, Tiger!" said Anansi. "Can the stories be named after me now?"

"I keep my promises," said Tiger. "You can have the stories. And this one shall be called The First Anansi Story!"

Traditional African folktale, retold by Richard Blythe and illustrated by Joanna Graham

My little pet spider

My spider has furry legs and a very
Big head with a very little brain inside it.
He lives in my front coat pocket
And sucks the end of my pencil.

John Kirkby   9 years old

SPIDERS

Meet an illustrator
MARTINA SELWAY

Martina Selway's job is drawing pictures for posters and for story books. She works at home, a big house near Hampton Court Palace, in London, where she lives with her husband, her two daughters, two cats, a dog and a hamster.

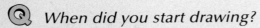

Q *When did you start drawing?*

A I went to lots of schools as my parents often moved house, so I always had to make new friends. Doing cartoons of the children, and the teachers, made people laugh, so I got to know everyone more quickly.

Q *What was your first drawing job?*

A A poster for London Transport on the parks you can visit. Then I did another one on street markets, like the one in Portobello Road.

Q *What paint do you use?*

A Dr Martin's Radiant Watercolours. They are really bright. If you mix them with just a little water, you get very strong colour.

Q *Do you draw some things differently?*

A Yes, I have several styles. Look at these two pictures. The one of the koala is very realistic. The one of Bronto the Brontosaurus is done in cartoon style. Which do you like best?

I like them both!

Q *Is it hard to draw the pictures?*

A I do them in pencil first. It can take four or five goes to get it right. I see the scene in my mind and then try to get it onto paper, juggling things around if I need to. For the stories about Fred, Kitty, Lucy and Barney, I drew a plan of their house so I knew where everything would go – a bit like the plan of a film set.

Q *Which is the best bit?*

A Doing the colour is the nicest part. I trace the pencil outlines onto white board and colour them in. I use ten different brushes – from size 8 to 000. Sometimes I use blotting paper to soak up the water or to dry a patch of colour.

Q *How many books have you done?*

A Over 150. I wrote the stories for *The Grunts* – they're a family of pigs – as well as doing the pictures.

WOW! More pigs!

I could never do that!

I like my work so much that sometimes I even forget to have a meal!

The Cock and the Dragon

You must have noticed, when the sun rises in the morning, how all the birds sing the most beautiful songs. All except the Cock, and he makes an ear-splitting noise, just as if he were angry about something. Well, he is.

Long ago, in ancient China, Cocks sang pleasant songs, like the other birds. They were happy and contented because they had beautiful feathers and magnificent horns which swept back from the sides of their shining heads.

One day, near a Chinese farmyard, a Dragon came flapping
and flaming through the sky. He had knobs and scales and
claws, eyes like plates, long waving whiskers and a fine
flowing mane. But no horns. So when he saw a Cock with
such fine horns he was terribly envious.

Down he swooped, close to the Cock. "Hrummph!" he
roared, as quietly as he could.

"If that means good morning," said the Cock, "then good
morning to you too."

"Lend me your horns," said the Dragon. "I am off to pay my
respects to the dragon gods, and horns are just what I need.
Please," he added, "dragons really should have horns, you
know!"

"How do I know you will bring them back?" asked the Cock.

"You can trust me," said the Dragon.

"Yes, you can trust him," said a little worm nearby.

"Very well," said the Cock. "But be sure you bring my horns back by this evening."

"I agree!" said the Dragon.

And so the Dragon took the Cock's horns. He patted the little worm, flapped his wings, blew smoke down his nose, and roared into the sky.

And never came back. Never! The Cock was very angry. Next morning he got up early. He poked about until he found the worm, and ate it out of temper. Then, he started shouting: "Bring back my horns!" Every morning, and sometimes during the day, he would shout the same thing.

It was hopeless. But the Cocks have not given up yet, and you can still hear that noisy shout of theirs: "Bring back my horns! Bring back my horns!"

Traditional Chinese folktale,
retold by Richard Blythe and
illustrated by Ian Penney

SPECIAL DAYS

CHINESE NEW YEAR

The Chinese New Year
begins with the first new moon
between 21st January and 19th February.
It is a family celebration, a time for visiting
friends and relatives . . . . . and for buying new clothes!

During the celebrations there is a
huge, colourful procession which is led
by a long, fantastic dragon made of silk and
velvet. The dragon weaves its way slowly through
the excited crowds to the music of
cymbols, drums and firecrackers.

Chinese New Year
is celebrated like this in many
countries where there are
large Chinese
communities.

Why is each Chinese New Year named after an animal?

Legend tells how an ancient Chinese teacher, Buddha, honoured the twelve animals who accepted his invitation to a party to celebrate the New Year.

Buddha named a year after each animal. To decide the order of the animals after which each year should be named, a race across a wide river was arranged.

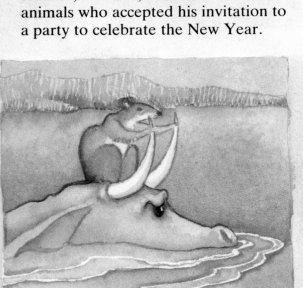

The clever Rat hitched a ride on the Ox's back, jumped off when they got across the river, raced to the finishing line, and won.

That is how the Year of the Rat became the first year of the Chinese calendar. You can see above how all the others followed in order.

William Shakespeare, the playwright, was born in the year of the Rat.

The Queen was born in a Tiger year.

Rat	1972	1984	1996
Ox	1973	1985	1997
Tiger	1974	1986	1998
Rabbit	1975	1987	1999
Dragon	1976	1988	2000
Snake	1977	1989	2001
Horse	1978	1990	2002
Goat	1979	1991	2003
Monkey	1980	1992	2004
Rooster	1981	1993	2005
Dog	1982	1994	2006
Pig	1983	1995	2007

Prince Philip was born in the year of the Rooster.

January

1st New Year's Day

6th Epiphany*

7th Christmas Day for Eastern Orthodox

26th Australia Day

Festivals whose dates vary

Makar Sankranti – a Hindu festival

New Year for Trees – a Jewish festival when new trees are planted

*On January 6th, Christians celebrate Twelfth Night or Epiphany. This was the night when the Magi (Wise Men) arrived to see the baby Jesus.

February

4th Sri Lanka National Day

6th Waitangi Day for New Zealanders

11th Japanese National Day

14th St Valentine's Day

Festivals whose dates vary

Chinese New Year*

Shrove Tuesday – Pancake Day!

*Chinese families celebrate the New Year with a colourful procession, fire crackers and parties.

March

1st St David's Day – Welsh National D

17th St Patrick's Day – Irish National Day

25th Greek Independence Day

Festivals whose dates vary

Holi – Hindu spring festival

Purim – a Jewish festival

Mother's Day

Easter

Ramadan – a Muslim fast*

*Ramadan is a time of fasting and prayer for Muslims. For a whole month, food and drink are not allowed between dawn and sunset. (Muslim festivals follow a lunar calendar and occur during different seasons over the years.)

April

1st April Fools' Day

23rd St George's Day
– English National
Day✱

13th or 14th
Baisakhi Mela
– a Sikh festival

**Festivals whose
dates vary**

Passover – Jewish spring
festival

Ching Ming – Chinese
spring festival

Buddha's birthday
– a Buddhist festival

Eid-ul-Fitr – a Muslim
feast celebrating the end
of Ramadan

May

1st May Day✱
1st Labour Day

**Festivals whose
dates vary**

Ascension Day
– a Christian festival

Pentecost (Whitsun)

The Whit Walks
– a traditional north of
England celebration

Shavuot – a Jewish festival
marking the receiving of
the Torah (Testament)

June

2nd Italian National Day
– celebrated by
Britain's Italian
community

23rd Midsummer's Eve

**Festivals whose
dates vary**

Ratha Yatra
– a Hindu festival

Well Dressing
– a Derbyshire custom✱

✱St George is
the patron
saint of
England.
Legend tells
how the knight,
George, rescued
a princess from
an evil dragon.

✱May Day is celebrated in
many villages of Britain by
dancing around a maypole.
The prettiest girl is chosen
as the May Queen. The
ceremony marks the
beginning of Spring
and the blossoming
of flowers.

✱In the county of
Derbyshire, the custom
of decorating wells with
flowers in religious scenes,
remains from the early belief
that evil spirits lived in the water.
The holy scenes kept the
evil spirits away.

Festivals

July

4th American Independence Day

5th Tynwald – The ceremony to open the Isle of Man parliament

12th Northern Ireland's Protestant community celebrate the Battle of the Boyne

15th St Swithin's Day

Festivals whose dates vary

Tisha B'Av – a Jewish fast

Raksha Bandhan – a Hindu family celebration✱

Eid-ul-Adha – a Muslim festival

✱In July, Hindus celebrate Raksha Bandhan. On this day, girls tie colourful wristbands of cotton or silk on to their brothers' wrists. This shows the protection that brothers should give to their sisters.

August

15th Indian Independence Day

Festivals whose dates vary

Welsh National Eisteddford – a festival of Welsh song and dance

Janamashtami – Hindus remember the birthday of Krishna

Notting Hill Carnival – London's West Indian community celebrate the traditions of Trinidad and Tobago

✱The West Indian community in London held their first small carnival in 1965. Since then it has become an annual event, with dazzling costumes and steel bands.

Septembe

29th Michaelmas Day – the Christian festiv of St Michael

Festival whose dates vary

Fishermen's Walk – the Scottish fishermen's harvest festival

Yom Kippur – Jewish Day of Atonement ✱

Dassehra – a Hindu festival celebrating the triumph of good over evil

✱ Yom Kippur, the Jewish Day of Atonement, is the day when Jews ask forgiveness for their sins during the past year. The ram's horn reminds Jews of when Abraham sacrificed a ram instead of his son, Isaac.

nd Parties

October

20th Oyster Day — Essex oyster fishermen celebrate the charter presented by Richard I

31st Hallowe'en — ancient Druids' festival *

Festivals whose dates vary

Divali — Festival of Lights (Hindu and Sikh)

Sukkot — Jewish harvest festival

Kathina — Buddhist present-giving festival

British harvest festival

*At Hallowe'en, bonfires used to be lit on hill tops to frighten away witches and other evil spirits. Today, Hallowe'en is a party time, with children dressing up as witches and playing games such as "bob apple".

November

1st All Saints Day

2nd All Souls Day

5th Guy Fawkes Night (Bonfire Night) *

30th St Andrew's Day — Scottish National Day

Festivals whose dates vary

Remembrance Sunday

Thanksgiving Day — American celebration

Guru Nanak's birthday — Sikhs remember the founder of their religion

*On 5th November, Guy Fawkes was captured while trying to blow up the Houses of Parliament. In 1606, the government decided that this day should be remembered with bonfires and fireworks.

December

21st Forefathers' Day — celebrates the first British settlers landing in America.

24th Western Christmas Eve

25th Western Christmas Day *

26th St Stephen's Day (Boxing Day)

31st New Year's Eve

Festivals whose dates vary

Hanukah — Jewish festival of lights

*On 25th December, Christians throughout the world celebrate the birth of Jesus Christ, the founder of their religion. Jesus was born in Bethlehem 2000 years ago.

How the Elephant Became

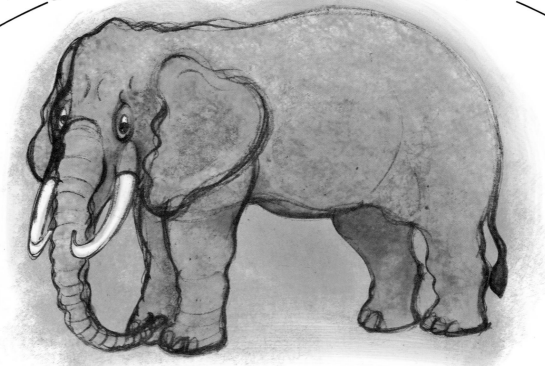

The unhappiest of all the creatures was Bombo.
Bombo didn't know what to become. At one
time he thought he might make a fairly good
horse. At another time he thought that perhaps he
was meant to be a kind of bull. But it was no
good. Not only the horses, but all the other
creatures too, gathered to laugh at him when he
tried to be a horse. And when he tried to be a bull,
the bulls just walked away shaking their heads.

"Be yourself," they all said.

Bombo sighed. That's all he ever heard: "Be
yourself. Be yourself." What was himself? That's
what he wanted to know.

So most of the time he just stood, with sad eyes, letting the wind blow his ears this way and that, while the other creatures raced around him and above him, perfecting themselves.

"I'm just stupid," he said to himself. "Just stupid and slow and I shall never become anything."

That was his main trouble, he felt sure. He was much too slow and clumsy — and so big! None of the other creatures were anywhere near so big. He searched hard to find another creature as big as he was, but there was not one. This made him feel all the more silly and in the way.

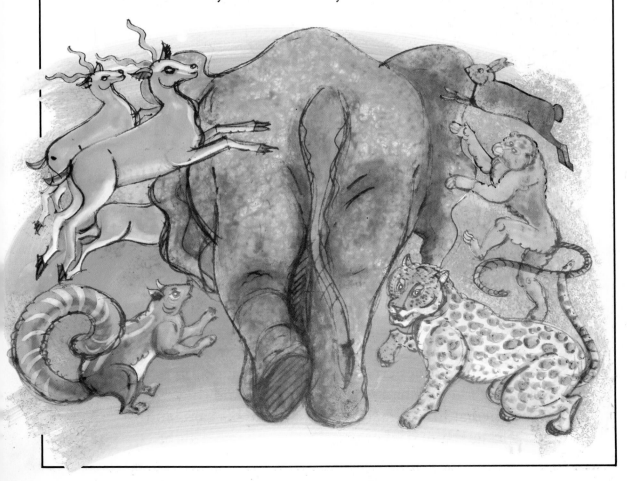

But this was not all. He had great ears that
flapped and hung, and a long, long nose. His nose
was useful. He could pick things up with it. But
none of the other creatures had a nose anything
like it. They all had small neat noses, and they
laughed at his. In fact, with that, and his ears, and
his long white sticking-out tusks, he was a sight.

As he stood, there was a sudden thunder of hooves. Bombo looked up in alarm.

"Aside, aside, aside!" roared a huge voice. "We're going down to drink."

Bombo managed to force his way backwards into a painful clump of thorn-bushes, just in time to let Buffalo charge past with all his family. Their long black bodies shone, their curved horns tossed, their tails screwed and curled, as they pounded down towards the water in a cloud of dust. The earth shook under them.

"There's no doubt," said Bombo, "who they are. If only I could be as sure of what I am as Buffalo is of what he is."

Then he pulled himself together.

"To be myself," he said aloud, "I shall have to do something that no other creature does. Lion roars and pounces, and Buffalo charges up and down bellowing. Each of these creatures does something that no other creature does. So. What shall I do?"

He thought hard for a minute.

Then he lay down, rolled over on to his back, and waved his four great legs in the air. After that he stood on his head and lifted his hind legs straight up as if he were going to sunburn the soles of his feet. From this position, he lowered himself back on to his four feet, stood up and looked round. The others should soon get to know me by that, he thought.

Nobody was in sight, so he waited until a pack of wolves appeared on the horizon. Then he began again. On to his back, his legs in the air, then on to his head, and his hind legs straight up.

"Phew!" he grunted, as he lowered himself. "I shall need some practice before I can keep this up for long."

31

When he stood up and looked round him this second time, he got a shock. All the animals were round him in a ring, rolling on their sides with laughter.

"Do it again! Oh, do it again!" they were crying, as they rolled and laughed. "Do it again. I shall die with laughter. Oh, my sides, my sides!"

Bombo stared at them in horror.

After a few minutes the laughter died down.

"Come on!" roared Lion. "Do it again and make us laugh. You look so silly when you do it."

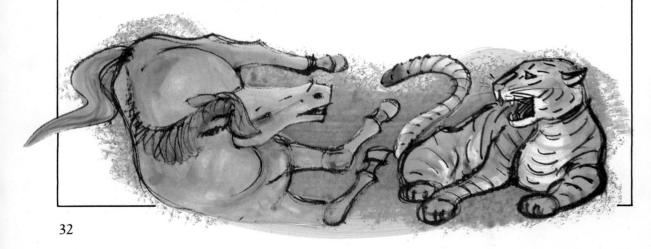

But Bombo just stood. This was much worse than imitating some other animal. He had never made them laugh so much before.

He sat down and pretended to be inspecting one of his feet, as if he were alone. And, one by one, now that there was nothing to laugh at, the other animals walked away, still chuckling over what they had seen.

"Next show same time tomorrow!" shouted Fox, and they all burst out laughing again.

Bombo sat, playing with his foot, letting the tears trickle down his long nose.

Well, he'd had enough. He'd tried to be himself, and all the animals had laughed at him.

That night he waded out to a small island in the
middle of the great river that ran through the
forest. And there, from then on, Bombo lived
alone, seen by nobody but the little birds and a
few beetles.

One night, many years later, Parrot suddenly
screamed and flew up into the air above the trees.
All his feathers were singed. The forest was on
fire.

Within a few minutes, the animals were
running for their lives. Jaguar, Wolf, Stag, Cow,
Bear, Sheep, Cockerel, Mouse, Giraffe — all were
running side by side and jumping over each other
to get away from the flames. Behind them, the
fire came through the treetops like a terrific red
wind.

"Oh dear! Oh dear! Our houses, our children!"
cried the animals.

Lion and Buffalo were running along with the
rest.

"The fire will go as far as the forest goes, and
the forest goes on for ever," they cried, and ran
with sparks falling into their hair. On and on they
ran, hour after hour, and all they could hear was
the thunder of the fire at their tails.

On into the middle of the next day, and still they were running.

At last they came to the wide, deep, swift river. They could go no farther. Behind them the fire boomed as it leapt from tree to tree. Smoke lay so thickly over the forest and the river that the sun could not be seen. The animals floundered in the shallows at the river's edge, trampling the banks to mud, treading on each other, coughing and sneezing in the white ashes that were falling thicker than thick snow out of the cloud of smoke. Fox sat on Sheep and Sheep sat on Rhinoceros.

They all set up a terrible roaring, wailing, crying, howling, moaning sound. It seemed like the end of the animals. The fire came nearer, bending over them like a thundering roof, while the black river swirled and rumbled beside them.

Out on his island stood Bombo, admiring the fire which made a fine sight through the smoke with its high spikes of red flame. He knew he was quite safe on his island. The fire couldn't cross that great stretch of water very easily.

At first he didn't see the animals crowding low by the edge of the water. The smoke and ash were too thick in the air. But soon he heard them. He recognised Lion's voice shouting:

"Keep ducking yourselves in the water. Keep your fur wet and the sparks will not burn you."

And the voice of Sheep crying:

"If we duck ourselves we're swept away by the river."

And the other creatures — Gnu, Ferret, Cobra, Partridge, crying:

"We must drown or burn. Good-bye, brothers and sisters!"

It certainly did seem like the end of the animals.

Without a pause, Bombo pushed his way into the water. The river was deep, the current heavy and fierce, but Bombo's legs were both long and strong. Burnt trees, that had fallen into the river higher up and were drifting down, banged against him, but he hardly felt them.

In a few minutes he was coming up into shallow water towards the animals. He was almost too late. The flames were forcing them, step by step, into the river, where the current was snatching them away.

Lion was sitting on Buffalo,
Wolf was sitting on Lion,
Wildcat on Wolf,
Badger on Wildcat,
Cockerel on Badger,
Rat on Cockerel,
Weasel on Rat,
Lizard on Weasel,
Tree-Creeper on Lizard,
Harvest Mouse on Tree-Creeper,
Beetle on Harvest Mouse,
Wasp on Beetle,
and on top of Wasp, Ant,
gazing at the
raging flames through
his spectacles and covering
his ears from their roar.

When the animals saw Bombo looming through the smoke, a great shout went up:
"It's Bombo! It's Bombo!"
All the animals took up the cry:
"Bombo! Bombo!"
Bombo kept coming closer. As he came, he sucked up water in his long silly nose and squirted it over his back, to protect himself from the heat and the sparks.

Then, with the same long, silly nose he reached out and began to pick up the animals, one by one, and seat them on his back.

"Take us!" cried Mole.

"Take us!" cried Monkey.

He loaded his back with the creatures that had hooves and big feet; then he told the little clinging things to cling on to the great folds of his ears. Soon he had every single creature aboard. Then he turned and began to wade back across the river, carrying all the animals of the forest towards safety.

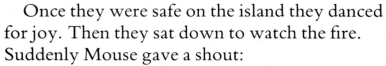

Once they were safe on the island they danced for joy. Then they sat down to watch the fire. Suddenly Mouse gave a shout:

"Look! The wind is bringing sparks across the river. The sparks are blowing into the island trees. We shall burn here too."

As he spoke, one of the trees on the edge of the island crackled into flames. The animals set up a great cry and began to run in all directions.

"Help! Help! Help! We shall burn here too!"

But Bombo was ready. He put those long silly tusks of his, that he had once been so ashamed of, under the roots of the burning tree and heaved it into the river. He threw every tree into the river till the island was bare. The sparks now fell on to the bare torn ground, where the animals trod them out easily. Bombo had saved them again.

Next morning the fire had died out at the river's edge. The animals on the island looked across at the smoking, blackened plain where the forest had been. Then they looked round for Bombo.

He was nowhere to be seen.

"Bombo!" they shouted. "Bombo!" And listened to the echo.

But he had gone.

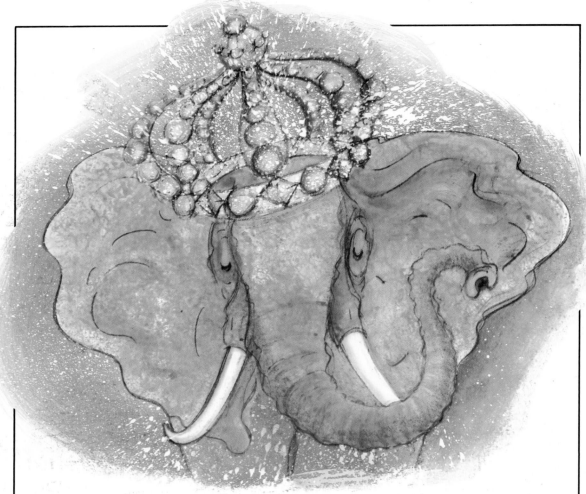

He is still very hard to find. Though he is huge and strong, he is very quiet.

But what did become of him in the end? Where is he now?

Ask any of the animals, and they will tell you:

"Though he is shy, he is the strongest, the cleverest, and the kindest of all the animals. He can carry anything and he can push anything down. He can pick you up in his nose and wave you in the air. We would make him our king if we could get him to wear a crown."

Written by Ted Hughes, illustrated by Wendy Leech

Feel like starting a restaurant for elephants?
Here's the kind of menu you'd need for...

JUMBO'S Dine-Inn

Menu

Lunch (for one)

12 kg of carrots
15 loaves of bread
1 bale of lucerne hay
10 kg of apples
bamboo leaves
some thin branches
(from a deciduous tree)
100 litres of fresh water
(available in 400 cups, 10 buckets
or one bath)

CUSTOMERS PLEASE NOTE

We are very happy for you to have a wash in your drinking water, but please don't splash the waitress.

A patch of dirt is provided outside the back door for throwing over yourself to help you get rid of those irritating insects that insist on living on elephants' skin. You see, we know how an itchy back spoils one's appetite!

WHERE DID ELEPHANTS COME FROM ?

Like all other animals, elephants have ancestors who lived on earth long, long ago. Some of these early elephant-like creatures died out. Others kept changing slowly as earth's climate and the plants growing on it changed also.

At some time elephants as we know them arrived in Africa and India, but no one can say for sure exactly when.

They now live in southern India, Assam, Nepal, Burma, peninsular Malaysia, southern China, Sri Lanka, Sumatra, Borneo and Africa south of the Sahara.

Pliocene

10,000,000 years ago

First came the Mastodon or straight-tusked elephant.

It lived in Europe, Asia, Africa and America.

Our human ancestors were alive at this time.

Pleistocene or Ice Ages

Next came the woolly Mammoth. Fossils have been found in Europe, northern Asia and America.

It lived at the same time as the sabre-toothed tiger.

Some of our human ancestors were living in caves at this time. They used fire to cook their food. They often painted pictures of the Mammoth on their cave walls.

Mammoths seem to have died out during one of the Ice Ages. There were several Ice Ages during this period.

Recent

25,000 years ago

It is not certain where elephants first appeared, but early fossils have been found in Africa and India. Today, African elephants are much bigger than the Indian ones and have bigger tusks.

This period includes the Stone Age (Paleolithic). By now humans had learned to use stone tools and weapons.

49

Lohimi the baby elephant

Lohimi was born at Circus Knie in Switzerland. Her mother's name is Claudy. Maxi, her father, came from Mary Chipperfield's Circus in England.

Here is Lohimi just 30 minutes after she was born! She was 97 centimetres high and weighed 125 kilograms. Six months later, she was 136 centimetres high and weighed 360 kilograms.

It takes 20 months for an elephant to grow inside its mother before it is born. This is the longest gestation period for any mammal. Humans take nine months and mice take only 17 days.

Lohimi will keep on growing until she is about 20 years old. Then she could measure 300 centimetres high at the shoulders and weigh 3000 kilograms. Asian elephants can live to be over 60 and mother elephants usually have their first calf between 16 and 20 years of age.

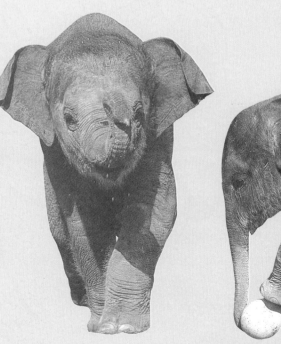

Elephants spend 18 out of 24 hours eating, and they can drink 136 litres of water a day. When the weather is cold, the water has to be specially heated for them.

The Taniwha

This is a story of a Maori water monster called the Taniwha.

This Taniwha lived in the Bay of Plenty in the North Island of New Zealand. That is where you will find Cape Runaway.

The story was written by Cathie Penetito and illustrated by Robert Jahnke.

Once a little boy climbed to the top of Tihirau. He saw a strange canoe sailing into the bay.

It was bigger than his father's canoe,
bigger than the chief's canoe,
bigger than any canoe he had ever seen.

He set off to tell his father. He was in such a hurry that he took a short cut to his home.

He went down through a deep dark valley with a deep dark cave. And in that cave there lived a terrible frightening Taniwha.

The little boy was so frightened that he squealed as he crept past the Taniwha's cave.

"Eiih! Eiih!"

With a roar and a scream the Taniwha woke up and came crashing out through the cave. He scratched at his horrible head with his horrible hands and thrashed his long tail about.

"Who woke me up!" he shouted.

"I did," said the little boy in a little voice. "Please don't eat me up! I'm hurrying home to tell my people about the strange canoe in the bay. Please don't eat me! I'll never, never come this way again."

"Very well," said Taniwha. "I won't eat you today. But if you wake me again I'll bite you into small pieces for my tea!"

56

And with a mighty roar the Taniwha crawled back into his cave.

The little boy trembled and shook and ran through the deep dark valley to his home as quickly as he could.

"Eiih! Eiiih! Eii!"

He met his father at the fence.

"Papa! I've seen a strange sight. There's a strange canoe in the bay. It's bigger than your canoe,

bigger than the chief's canoe,

bigger than any canoe I've ever seen!"

They went straight to the chief and the chief told his strongest warriors to launch their biggest canoe. They pushed off from the shore and paddled out to meet the strange canoe.

It was a strange sight. A huge canoe with pale men aboard, wearing strange clothes. The warriors were frightened but they paddled straight towards the ship making fierce faces and looking as brave as they could.

Captain Cook saw their fierce faces and was frightened.

"Man the cannon" he cried.

"Light the fuse!"

And the cannon ball went off with an enormous

BANG!

And who heard it? Ah yes. Taniwha! He woke with a roar and a scream, scratched his horrible head with his horrible hands and thrashed his long tail about.

"Who woke me up again!" he shouted.

He looked out from the mouth of his cave and there below him in the bay he saw the large black cannon ball that made the BANG that woke him up. And he saw the strange canoe that had fired the cannon that had sent the cannon ball whistling through the air.

"Eeeii!" he yelled.

He flew down to the bay and caught the cannon ball in his horrible hands. With a roar and a scream he threw the cannon ball right back at the strange canoe.

"Don't wake me up again!"

Captain Cook saw the cannon ball hurtling towards his ship.

"Hoist the sail!" he called. "Row!" he called.

"Turn about!" he yelled.

That night, Captain Cook charted Cape Runaway on his
big map. The horrible Taniwha smiled in his sleep in
his cave.

    And the little boy and his father
                    and the chief
                    and all the warriors
                                    smiled happily
and went to sleep in their house at Whangaparaoa*.

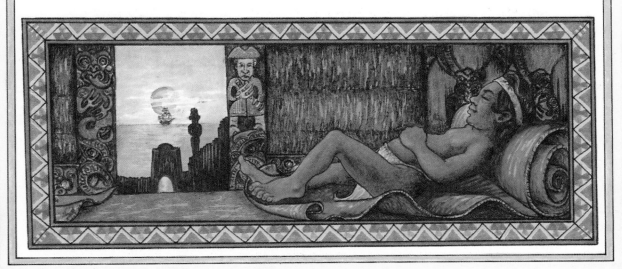

*Pronounced "Fahngah-parah-aw-a" (all syllables unstressed).
It is a small bay, and the name means "bay of whales".

Who was Captain Cook?

James Cook was born in 1728 in Yorkshire. He started work as an errand boy but he wanted to be a sailor. As often as he could, he went down to Whitby harbour to watch the ships.

His first sailing job was on the coal-carrying ship, *Freelove*. He soon became interested in navigation and began to study it.

Later he joined the Royal Navy and saw active service in the Seven Years' War with France.

In 1769, as Captain of the *Endeavour*, he sailed to New Zealand to chart its coastline.

In 1770, after his ship had been damaged on the coral of the Great Barrier Reef, Cook landed in Australia and claimed it for Britain. Captain Cook spent the rest of his life exploring the Pacific Ocean islands. On one of these, Maui, he was killed by the islanders in 1779.

Words to chant

Glossary

ancestors *(p. 48)*
members of the same family who lived a long time ago

ancient *(p. 14)*
long ago; very old

bellowing *(p. 30)*
making a loud, deep sound

floundered *(p. 36)*
moved awkwardly and helplessly

fossil *(p. 49)*
a hardened part or print of an animal or plant of long ago, that has been preserved in rock, ice, etc

Glossary continues on page 64

gestation (*p. 52*)
the time when a baby
or animal is growing
inside its mother's body
before it is born

hoist (*p. 60*)
to raise or lift up
something

imitating (*p. 33*)
copying the behaviour,
appearance, speech,
etc of someone or
something

Maori (*p. 54*)
aboriginal people of
New Zealand

navigation (*p. 62*)
planning the route of
a ship, plane, etc

pounded (*p. 29*)
moved with quick,
heavy steps which
made a dull sound

swift (*p. 36*)
fast